Original title:
The Attic of Dreams

Copyright © 2025 Creative Arts Management OÜ
All rights reserved.

Author: Rory Fitzgerald
ISBN HARDBACK: 978-1-80587-195-8
ISBN PAPERBACK: 978-1-80587-665-6

Celestial Promises in Cardboard

In a box marked 'fragile', stars reside,
They giggle with glee, so hard to hide.
A moonbeam ladder, stacked up high,
Whispers of candy clouds in the sky.

Aliens play poker, it's quite a sight,
With Martian chip stacks, what a delight!
They'll trade you a comet for some old cheese,
While black holes sing songs, sure to tease.

Staircases to Tomorrow

Up the spiral stairs of fantasies,
Wobbly steps made of jellybeans,
Each shift brings a giggle, a joyful leap,
To leap through time, not lose a sleep.

A cat in a top hat, oh what a show,
He juggles the sun while reading the snow.
Tick-tock, tick-tock, the clocks start to pop,
And candy canes grow, as dreams never stop.

Fragments of Daydreams

Floating whims in a teacup boat,
Sailing on giggles, that's quite the quote.
A lightbulb fish swims round and round,
While lollipop trees dance to the sound.

Whispers of laughter fill the air,
As rubber ducks form a merry fair.
In this land where nonsense reigns supreme,
Life's just a joke, a glorious dream!

The Gallery of Unseen Stories

Painted walls with tales untold,
Brush strokes of humor, bright and bold.
A sneeze turns to art, sparks will fly,
As giggles and snorts soar up to the sky.

There's a painting of socks that danced in pairs,
With secrets whispered under the stairs.
Each frame a snapshot, oh what a tease,
Laughter's the treasure in this gallery breeze.

Ghosts of Past Embraces

In corners lurk those silly socks,
I've lost the mates to all my flocks.
The old cat jokes, with fur so gray,
"Just keep your clothes, I'll take the pay!"

Cobwebs dance like silly dreams,
Floating lightly on moonbeams.
They whisper tales of toys long tossed,
And every laugh, a memory lost.

Where Time Gathers Dust

Old clocks tick softly, running slow,
Time's a prankster, just for show.
It giggles at our frantic pace,
While dust bunnies do a silent race.

Books piled high in wild disarray,
Each title says, "Read me someday!"
The tales inside, they grin and tease,
A novel's got some tricks, if you please.

Hidden Treasures Beneath the Eaves

Beneath the beams, the secrets lie,
Old candy wrappers dare to fly.
Uncle Ted's joke book, oh what fun,
Each punchline lands, and then it's done!

A tricycle lost, with rust so grand,
Hopes of racing with friends, so planned.
It wobbles like my thoughts today,
But in this space, who cares, hooray!

The Silence of Unspoken Wishes

In quiet corners, dreams take flight,
Their giggles echo in the night.
A wish on paper, crumpled tight,
Whispers secrets, out of sight.

Lost socks plead with a funny grin,
"Please find me, mate, let's all begin!"
Yet here we sit, in silence bold,
As memories rattle, bright and cold.

The Dance of Dust and Time

In corners high, the dust bunnies prance,
They twirl and spin, in a whimsical dance.
With each little flick, they giggle and play,
As socks join hands in a fluffy ballet.

Old hats and shoes do the cha-cha cha,
While forgotten toys argue, 'Aren't we bizarre?'
The clocks tick-tock, in their jolly old chime,
In a world of whimsy, where laughter's prime.

The Unraveling of Stacks Forgotten

Books piled high, like a tower of dreams,
Whisper their tales, or so it seems.
But one sneaky tome does a backflip for fun,
While another sings songs of old times begun.

Old photo albums leap from the shelves,
To reveal their secrets, as if they were elves.
With smiles and frowns, they spin the old yarn,
In this world of memories, none can feel torn.

Whispers in Forgotten Corners

In the shadowy nooks, the critters collide,
A mouse in a tux, with a bird as his guide.
They plot a heist of a leftover crumb,
While giggles erupt from an old, squeaky drum.

An old chair complains of its creaks and its aches,
As the spiders debate on what kind of cakes.
With whispers so soft, they tickle the air,
Creating a symphony, both silly and rare.

Dusty Reflections in the Moonlight

Moonbeams dance on the shelves with glee,
As dust motes pirouette, wild and free.
Mirrors chuckle at the faces they see,
In this wacky world where all things agree.

A cat with a hat shares a joke with a broom,
As laughter erupts, lighting up the gloom.
In the glow of the night, misunderstandings grow,
In a spectacle of madness, the fun steals the show.

Echoing Dreams that Never Were

In a box of socks, a treasure lies,
A rubber chicken and a pair of eyes.
A yo-yo spins with perfect grace,
While shadows dance in a silly chase.

Forgotten hats with polka dots hang,
A trombone emits a funny clang.
The clock ticks backwards, what a sight!
Laughter echoes through the night.

A reindeer suit, a wig of blue,
In the chaos, there's always a clue.
A dance-off with a broom can be fun,
Who knew mischief could weigh a ton?

So welcome the improbable games we play,
In this quirky world, let's drift away.
With dreams collecting dust like old toys,
Let's be the clowns, the girls, and the boys.

Tattered Pages of Unseen Tales

Old books whisper with secrets rare,
Stories of emperors who lost their hair.
A pirate's map that leads to a sneeze,
And knights who joust with giant quiche.

A dragon with glitter, a cat in a hat,
Each page a puzzle, imagine that!
With crumpets and giggles in every line,
Writing tales over mugs of brine.

In corners, a raccoon plays chess,
With imaginary friends, oh such a mess!
Fictional worlds where nothing's quite right,
Imagination takes off, a joyful flight.

So gather the scraps and weave a new scheme,
On these tattered pages, let's laugh and dream.
For unseen tales are best when they twirl,
In the whimsical chaos of this silly whirl.

Veils of Memory and Moonlight

Moonbeams giggle through the cracks,
As forgotten legends come to relax.
A fairy riding a snail so slow,
Tells jokes that only the fireflies know.

With memories wrapped in sheets of grey,
They hop and skip like a cabaret.
Old socks with stories, a slipper with flair,
Dragons and donuts float in the air.

The moon, a joker, grins wide and bright,
Casting shadows that dance with delight.
Wind chimes tinkle sweet melodies,
Chasing giggles down the swaying trees.

So let's lift the veil and wander in glee,
In the glow of memories, so wild and free.
With every chuckle and every strand,
The night whispers secrets we all understand.

Spirals of Hope in Dusty Corners

In the corners where dust bunnies play,
Lie dreams that decided to stay.
A dinosaur dressed in a tutu bright,
Spins around under the soft candlelight.

Tangled yarns of laughter and cheer,
Each spiral a tale, drawing us near.
With hopes that flutter like butterflies,
And a symphony of silly sighs.

Old toys with wheels that won't stop,
Chasing the angles with a funny hop.
A kite of wishes stuck on the shelf,
Screaming, 'Come play, but do it yourself!'

So let's dance through the dust and the dreams,
In this world of wonder, nothing's as it seems.
With hopeful spirals that weave and entwine,
A collection of laughter, forever divine.

Lanterns of Enchanted Remembrance

In a box of old socks, I found a lost clown,
His nose honked 'hello' while tumbling down.
A dance with a broom, oh what a delight,
We spun and we twirled till we faded from sight.

A cat in a hat, with a smile made of cheese,
Told tales of the sky and how it can freeze.
He offered me cupcakes that sang as they baked,
And laughed 'til we cried at each sweet joke we faked.

Ceilings of Untamed Imagination

The ceiling grew legs and started to prance,
With walls that were giggling, they joined in the dance.
A lamp turned to light-up, a disco ball bright,
We grooved through the rooms in a whirl of delight.

On the shelf, a sock puppet wore a grand crown,
While giggling gnomes taped a new funny gown.
They painted the wallpaper with polka dot blobs,
And turned all the windows to colorful mobs.

Stories Scribbled on Cardboard

A book made of carton began to recite,
Tales of a dragon who couldn't take flight.
He wore fuzzy slippers and hummed a sweet tune,
While we battled his fears 'neath the glow of the moon.

With crayons on paper, we crafted a plot,
A pirate named Zeke who forgot what he sought.
His treasure was pizza, a cheesy delight,
We shared it with laughter through the breezy night.

Dreams Adrift in Celestial Attics

A spaceship of pillows took off with a cheer,
Alongside the stuffed bear who had nothing to fear.
They visited planets made of jelly and cheese,
And danced with the stars in a whimsical breeze.

On moons made of marshmallows, we leaped and we bounced,
While giggles erupted, the fun was pronounced.
With dreams flying high, we discovered a game,
Where wishes and laughter ignited the flame.

Twinkling Shadows of Youth

In corners where the dust bunnies dance,
A mouse steals a sneaker, oh what a chance!
Old toys giggle beneath the old beams,
As memories flutter like whimsical dreams.

Forgotten socks have a secret to tell,
Of childhood adventures, oh how they swell!
The echoes of laughter mix sweet with the brash,
While the cat starts a ruckus, a merry old clash.

A broken lamp whispers tales of delight,
As shadows perform in the soft moonlight.
A puzzle's missing piece lies in a shoe,
Who knew such chaos could come from a few?

So let this old space be our foolish retreat,
With laughter and quirks, life is never obsolete.
We'll treasure the mess and the giggles they bring,
For in silly mischief, our hearts will still sing.

Recollections in Rotted Frames

Old photographs grin from their warped little place,
With mustaches and pouts, a comical face.
Once a grand portrait, now a bit ruffled,
As the paint chips away, the characters shuffled.

On creaky old shelves, a rubber chicken lays,
Its laughter still echoes from long-ago days.
Dusty old hats piled ridiculously high,
As we ponder what happens when mice pass by.

A broken clock giggles, time's lost its way,
While cobwebs have formed in a curious bouquet.
The portraits watch us with eyes of surprise,
At the stories we tell through colorful lies.

In frames that have weathered the storm and the time,
We find joy in the chaos, a comical rhyme.
For every odd picture and confusion we've faced,
Reminds us that life can be humor embraced.

Guardians of the Overlooked

In shadowy corners where oddities dwell,
A stuffed bear in a tux sings us a swell.
With mismatched socks and a solo shoe,
This crew of the goofy always makes do.

The dust motes are guardians of laughter and cheer,
Warding off worries that slip in so near.
A rubber fish bobs on a shelf with a grin,
While giggles escape from boxes akin.

A juggler made out of throw pillows bright,
Hopes to entertain with a comical plight.
While cobwebs weave curtains that flail in the breeze,
Dusty old boxes hold secrets with ease.

So let's raise a toast to the quirky and absurd,
To the tales of the forgotten, never unheard.
For in this realms where the overlooked dwell,
Life's laughter and fun surely casts a spell.

The Heartbeats of Old Houses

In the nooks where the floorboards sing a tune,
Creaks and whispers harmonize with the moon.
The curtains wave gaily, a soft, silly dance,
Breathing stories of joy, if given a chance.

The windows are eyes peeking out from their plight,
While the kitchen croons softly with scents of delight.
The refrigerator hums a jolly old song,
As old recipes beckon, both quirky and strong.

In corners, the quirks of a life are laid bare,
Knickknacks in chaos, they all seem to stare.
A ladybug's laughter, where the floor meets the wall,
Reminds us that life can be funny after all.

So cherish the heartbeat, the giggle-filled space,
Where life's little silly moments dare to embrace.
For in every crevice, humor can thrive,
In the heart of old houses, we truly come alive.

Echoes of Childhood Laughter

In corners where dust bunnies play,
A tricycle waits for a brighter day.
With squeaky wheels and a rusty bell,
It's holding stories no one can tell.

A teddy bear wearing a cap,
Sips tea from a porcelain nap.
He winks and giggles, oh so bright,
Crafting adventures in the night.

Old toy soldiers stand at attention,
Waging wars without a mention.
A rubber duck in a sink parade,
Echoes of joy in a grand charade.

A kite with dreams hovers above,
Glimmers of laughter, a whisper of love.
Each memory dances, laughter sets free,
In this whimsical space, just you and me.

Shadows of Lost Tomorrows

A clock with no hands spins around,
Counting giggles that time has bound.
Each tick-tock holds a secret taught,
Of balloon animals and battles fought.

Pirate maps made of crumpled dreams,
Lead to treasure where laughter teems.
With Xs marking spots of delight,
Shadows prance in the soft moonlight.

A spaceship made of cardboard flew,
Past cotton clouds of pink and blue.
In its crew, we're all astronauts,
Zooming through laughter-filled plots.

Marbles roll and clatter about,
Building castles from a child's shout.
Within these walls, who needs tomorrows?
Only echoes, and a laugh that borrows.

Forgotten Trunks and Echoing Hopes

An old trunk creaks with tales to share,
Of mismatched socks and pirate flair.
Within its depths, treasures unsung,
Songs of silence, forever young.

A caped crusader with cardboard wings,
Soars through the attic, defying things.
With laughter that rounds each dusty bend,
Every odd trinket, a faithful friend.

A rubber band ball, oh so tall,
Bounces dreams with a goofy sprawl.
It holds the giggles of yesterdays,
And hopes that twinkle in whimsical ways.

Each memory spills like confetti bright,
Twirling round in the soft moonlight.
The past is a canvas we've painted right,
With echoes of joy that take flight.

Secrets Held Within Wooden Beams

Whispers linger in the rafters high,
As spider webs weave tales with a sigh.
An owl in the corner nods with glee,
Clutching secrets, just him and me.

A wooden chest of mismatched keys,
Unlocks giggles hidden in the breeze.
Each creak of the floor tells a story wide,
From pirate ships to a dinosaur ride.

A jigsaw puzzle with pieces askew,
Each shape a moment reflecting you.
When put together, they spark delight,
Creating a kaleidoscope of light.

The beams above are a storyteller's stage,
Reciting laughs from every age.
In shadows and dust, we find our way,
To secrets of joy that forever stay.

Whispers of Forgotten Skylights

Up high where dust bunnies twirl,
Old socks and lonely hats unfurl.
Winking stars peek through gaps bright,
They giggle softly in the night.

Crickets hold a raucous ball,
While moths attempt a daring crawl.
The chandelier's lost its charm,
Swinging 'round with a twitching arm.

Half a bicycle sits in repose,
An umbrella with stories to pose.
Each echo whispers, 'Take a ride!',
"Just don't forget to bring your pride!"

Memories dressed in tattered rags,
Jive and josh like silly brags.
Silly shoes stomp to a tune,
In the nook where mischief's strewn.

Shadows in the Dusty Corners

In the shadows, a gnome does prance,
With a belly laugh and a silly dance.
Cobbwebs dangle as he spins,
Stealing all the laughter wins.

A forgotten toy breaks out in cheer,
Exclaims, 'It's party time, my dear!'
Matchbox cars form a wild parade,
With giggles echoing through the glade.

Mice with caps gather round,
Swapping tales in squeaks and sounds.
Each corner holds a secret game,
Where shadows dance with laughter's name.

Dust bunnies play poker, hats askew,
With rusty screws as chips, who knew?
The night ignites with playful zest,
In corners where the fun won't rest.

Echoes of Hidden Memories

Squeaky shoes and a rusty bike,
Once rode into adventure's hike.
Now they sit, with dreams piled high,
Underneath the questioning sky.

Old photographs hang with a grin,
Dogs in costumes, where to begin?
The laughter trapped in the frames,
Whispers softly of silly games.

A violin with a broken string,
Hums a tune of forgotten swing.
In its case, a dance card sways,
Reminding all of long-lost days.

Echoes bounce like a curious cat,
Chasing memories, where are they at?
With every creak, they comic spree,
Twisting tales of history.

Lanterns of Longing

The lanterns glow with mismatched light,
Where wishes linger, oh what a sight!
Each flicker holds a giggle tight,
Of forgotten hopes that take to flight.

A rubber chicken makes its stand,
Joking 'round with a gentle hand.
With every flap, it brings a cheer,
For laughter thrives in yesteryear.

Illuminated in a silly scheme,
Framed by shadows, they gleam and beam.
Each corner bursts with playful flair,
In a world that's rich and rare.

So gather 'round and share a laugh,
In lantern light, we'll draft our path.
With giggles bright, we'll light the way,
In the joyful hues of endless play.

Dusty Dreams and Forgotten Schemes

In a corner lies a shoe,
Two mismatched, what a view!
A pair that couldn't dance,
Yet dreamed of a chance.

Beneath the beams, a hat so tall,
Worn by a cat that had a ball.
They planned to fly, around the town,
But tripped and tumbled down.

Old maps with paths all askew,
Show treasures that never grew.
Pirate dreams in crumpled scrolls,
Just like the muffins left in bowls.

An old clock chimes, but it's stuck,
Time forgot to add some luck.
Yet in this space of jumbled things,
Laughter's what the memory brings.

The Poetry of Unopened Boxes

Boxes stacked up high like towers,
Hiding secrets, dusty flowers.
They whisper tales of long-since days,
In wacky, wonderful, twisted ways.

One promises a fancy dress,
That turned into a feline mess.
A jester's hat, a rubber duck,
Each box tells tales of silly luck.

Beneath the lids, wild wonders bide,
A sock that claims to be a guide.
It laughs at fashions from the past,
While future styles come and go fast.

A puzzle piece that leads to nowhere,
Winks at those who stop and stare.
In gathering gloom, they spark delight,
In unopened boxes, dreams take flight.

Lament of Lost Hopes

Once a kite, bright and bold,
Now a scrap of tale untold.
It yearned to soar, but caught on trees,
Only to sway in the breeze.

Old trophies gather dust and grime,
For races lost to space and time.
Each brittle memory, a little gruff,
Whispers, "Winning was just too tough!"

Cookies baked but burnt to stone,
Crispy reminders we're not alone.
Beneath the laughs and playful hugs,
Lie the remnants of our fluffed shrugs.

Yet after all the boo-hooing fits,
The laughter sneaks through like comfy mitts.
Lost hopes may hide in shadows dim,
But funny tales keep spirits trim.

The Sighs of Yesteryears

A feather pen, once grand and proud,
Now scribbles tales beneath a shroud.
It dreams of poets, wordy and clear,
But writes more doodles filled with cheer.

Old photographs with faces blurred,
Captured moments of laughter stirred.
Supposing they were grand events,
But mostly just silly misadventures hence.

A gramophone that plays off-key,
Sings of yesterdays, wild and free.
Though notes are jumbled, strange and sweet,
They dance together to a quirky beat.

So let us sigh and giggle loud,
In memories lost, we stand so proud.
For every fumble, every stumble here,
Turns into laughter we hold dear.

Boxes of Unwritten Futures

In boxes stacked, a tale unfolds,
Of mismatched socks and toys of old.
A rubber duck with one lazy eye,
Is plotting schemes to learn to fly.

There's a sandwich from last July's feast,
Whispering tales like a party beast.
Old notes promise treasures untold,
While crayons argue over their bold.

A space warrior with wayward style,
Claims the loot with a goofy smile.
In the chaos, we might just find,
The laughter echoing in the mind.

So let's dive deep in this quirky chest,
Seeking out the laughter, we like best.
With every stumble, slip, and fall,
We craft a story, after all!

A Symphony of Forgotten Wishes

In corners dark, the wishes hum,
A chorus of things we've never done.
A broken guitar with invisible strings,
Sings of adventures and wild flings.

Dancing shoes, two sizes too small,
Twirl around as they start to brawl.
They stomp on floors with all their might,
Shrieking 'We'll dance till morning light!'

A jump rope's tale of double-dare,
Tangles with the stories in the air.
A pogo stick dreams of taking flight,
While squishy bears join in the night.

With giggles trapped in dusty drawers,
They weave a symphony of folklore.
Unraveled yarns spin tales of glee,
In a world where wishes run free!

Dust Motions in Twilight

The dust motes twirl like little sprites,
In fading hints of summer nights.
They dance a jig on sunbeams bright,
And giggle softly, out of sight.

An old broom waits for its grand debut,
Hoping to join in the dust-ball crew.
While shadows gather for a game,
Of hide-and-seek, without a name.

The couch now claims the precious prize,
A remote control that never lies.
It spins tales of channels long gone,
Where laughter lingered from dusk till dawn.

So watch the motes as they take their flight,
Spinning tales of mischief each night.
With every swirl, a giggle's sound,
In the twilight, joy is found!

Secrets Behind the Eaves

Up high where the cobwebs sprawl,
Secrets linger, both big and small.
There's a gnome in a tutu, dancing free,
Whispering jokes like a comical decree.

A squirrel's hat sewn from threadbare rags,
Leads a team of mismatched flags.
While feather dusters dream of fame,
They argue over who gets the name.

Parades of laundry, colors bright,
Tumble together in joyous flight.
Each sock cha-chas with a wiggle and sway,
Grooving in the attic ballet.

Those secrets hide a joke or two,
For laughter, dear friend, waits for you.
Within the eaves, where stories weave,
The fun begins, if you believe!

Journeys Beneath the Dust

In the corner, a globe spins fast,
A pirate hat, my time machine cast.
I ride a cat, in socks too big,
Adventure calls, let's dance a jig!

Old toys whisper secrets of yore,
While dust bunnies plot their uproar.
Under the stairs, a treasure chest,
I can't find socks, but I find a quest!

Maps of candy land, oh the thrill!
With gummy bears, we'll climb a hill.
A rubber band slingshot made me king,
In this mad kingdom, let chaos sing!

The clock ticks loud, it's time to play,
I lost my shoes, they ran away.
But fear not, for here I reign,
A dusty monarch, oh what a gain!

Lighthouses of the Past

A rusted lamp shines way too bright,
Underneath it, shadows take flight.
I found a map to a pirate's stew,
But it leads to socks and a lost shoe!

Candles lit in a sea of books,
A ladybug gives judgmental looks.
The lighthouse beams through cobwebbed air,
As I navigate a teddy's chair!

Oh, the stories these walls could tell,
Of lost dreams and a jolly yell.
They guide the lost to fantasy lands,
With secret paths and sticky hands.

A spider spins tales, ever so sly,
While I plot my escape, oh my!
Lighthouses gleam with mischief's glow,
In this wild adventure, let's go, go, go!

Faded Photographs of Possibility

Old snapshots hang like whispered dreams,
A laughing cat, or so it seems.
In a world of sepia tones,
Lie wild adventures on paper bones.

A leaping frog with a top hat fine,
In this gallery of stray confine.
An owl wearing glasses reads a page,
In these frames, we launch a stage!

My childhood friends in crazy poses,
In muddied boots and wilted roses.
Climbing trees, we knew no bounds,
Creating worlds where laughter sounds.

With every click, a story spun,
Mischief found in the midday sun.
These faded snapshots, life's sweet tease,
Picture perfect moments, if you please!

Cardboard Castles Under the Stars

In the yard, kingdoms made of scraps,
A dragon sneezes, oh, it flaps!
With knights in pajamas, armed with spoons,
We battle shadows and glow-in-the-dark moons.

The walls are painted with dreams astray,
Where ninja hamsters come out to play.
Our crowns are made of cereal boxes,
While ruler of giggles stacks up the flockses!

A cardboard bridge leads to nowhere bold,
With maps scribbled in crayon so old.
We sail through valleys of marshmallow cream,
In this wacky dream, we reign supreme!

Stars above twinkle in sheer delight,
As we hop on clouds, ready for flight.
In our cardboard kingdoms, we are free,
Just silly knights laughing joyfully!

The Horizon of Yesterdays

Old shoes that squeak and squeal,
Dust bunnies dance, oh what a deal.
Time's secrets hide in every nook,
Where memories smile, and giggles cook.

Jars of marbles, a colorful sea,
The future's locked in a shiny key.
Rusted toys with tales to tell,
In painted corners, they weave their spell.

A hat that once fit a giant cat,
Now rests on a moldy old mat.
Socks that wandered far too long,
In the land of mismatched, they belong.

Through windows cracked, the sunlight beams,
As laughter echoes in flickering dreams.
Jumping jacks freeze in mid-air chase,
While yesterday's joy paints every space.

Silhouettes of What Once Was

A tricycle wheels with a squeaky song,
Once rode so proud, where can it belong?
Beneath the dust, a lost dog barks,
Chasing shadows of old playground larks.

A teddy bear lost its fluffy flair,
Plotting revenge, but who would care?
The clock ticks funny, time's lost its race,
Each tick a giggle, a silly embrace.

Puzzles missing pieces, a quirky sight,
Cornered in cobwebs, they take flight.
Laughter lingers like paint gone dry,
Chasing memories as time drifts by.

Hats stacked high, like a circus clown,
Pile them up, let's turn this frown.
With every step, a route to the past,
In this playful maze, we're free at last.

Whispers in the Twilight Trunks

A trunk of treasures, where dust bunnies roam,
Little hands search for a piece of home.
Socks that have tangoed with shoes of flair,
Whisper of journeys, light as air.

Old costumes twirl in a ghostly play,
A pirate, a princess, come out to say:
"Let's raise the sails, the world's our stage,
With laughter and joy, let's turn the page."

Letters with ink that has faded away,
Tell stories of kids who would laugh and play.
They whisper secrets to the cobwebs' throng,
In the twilight stillness, where mischief grows strong.

A cat's old collar, a puppy's bow tie,
Scribbled dreams on a napkin nearby.
Each item holds laughter, memories gleam,
In this magical place where wonders seem.

Echoes from the Wooden Beams

Up in the rafters, where dust motes dance,
Echoes of children, lost in a trance.
With puppet shows and laughter in tow,
Timeless antics that still seem to glow.

A leap over shadows, a giggle turns loud,
As toys hold court, in a jolly crowd.
With every creak and crack of the wood,
The past sneaks up, it's boldly misunderstood.

Boots that have marched through mud and mischief,
Lurking around, creating a rift.
In playful banter, they spin around,
As echoes of laughter in beams abound.

Ticklish whispers and secrets galore,
In a time capsule filled with joy we explore.
Beneath every beam, a tale waits to gleam,
In this wacky world of our wildest dream.

The Clouded Canvas of Thought

In a corner, a hat with a feather,
It always twists in stormy weather.
A brush dipped in jellybeans bright,
Painting giggles that dance in the light.

An easel that wobbles like a duck,
Slicing ideas that run out of luck.
Each stroke is a tickle, a laugh's quick tease,
A canvas of chaos that never would freeze.

Smudged clouds of pink, purples on spree,
Splatters of laughter, all for the key.
Creativity's cranky, but oh so grand,
With paint on my fingers, I still take a stand.

A masterpiece waits where no one can see,
A madcap world of imaginary glee.
It's silly, it's strange, and full of delight,
A laugh in each corner, a joy in each sight.

Moonlight Through Weathered Glass

Glimmering cracks whisper secrets at night,
Where shadows mingle in playful fright.
The moon's just a prankster behind the pane,
Shooting beams of silver that cause me to feign.

Glasses of lemonade stacked up high,
Reflecting a circus that dances nearby.
My cat in a cape thinks he's on the stage,
Dancing to tunes that they'll never gauge.

Each sip feels like a trip down the lane,
To a world where it's normal to sing in the rain.
Old frames that are full of collector's despair,
Capture the moments of laughter in air.

With giggles of dust, they spin and they twirl,
Caught in a gleam, they whirl and they whirl.
The night feels alive, in a playful glow,
Where whispers and chuckles together bestow.

Time-Traveled Trunks

An old trunk snaps open, a pop and a plop,
Surprises jump out, like popcorn that hops.
From jackets of velvet to shoes that squeak,
Each piece has a tale, though some feel quite weak.

A hat from a party, a globe full of dreams,
Worn out from travel, bursting at seams.
Each item a ticket to ages gone by,
With laughter that echoes, oh my, oh my!

A treasure of socks, all mismatched and bright,
They wiggle and giggle, just pure silly fright.
With whispers of history tangled in thread,
These relics are silly, but funny instead.

Time-traveling items that hold whimsy's hand,
A magic that giggles with each twist and strand.
These trunks are alive, with laughter they cling,
To moments forgotten but always bring spring.

Scrolls of Forgotten Adventures

Rolled up like candies, with secrets to keep,
Each scroll has a story that makes me leap.
Dragons on scooters, knights with a joke,
A world where the silliness never goes broke.

With crayon-clad maps and treasure so sweet,
X marks the spot of a candy retreat.
A pirate in flip-flops, a parrot that sings,
In these scrolls of laughter, absurdity springs.

A heist for some cheese in a kingdom of bread,
Where mice hold the keys and lead us ahead.
Every twist in the tale is a laugh on the run,
With adventure so silly, it's hard not to stun.

These pages of whimsy, with histories bright,
Whirl through the ages, in colorful flight.
Each sentence a giggle, a sigh, and a cheer,
Forgotten adventures still bring joy near.

Entropy of Past Illusions

In the corner, a hat sits tall,
With a rabbit, who seems to call.
Dust collects on memories bright,
While socks argue, who stole the light.

Old photos giggle, wearing frowns,
Telling tales of clumsy clowns.
Mismatched shoes tap a silly beat,
As the clock falls asleep on its feet.

Jars of marbles roll in retreat,
While crayons conspire for a sweet treat.
A wooden horse laughs at the wall,
Wishing it could join the ball.

Ghosts of laughter swirl like fog,
Tickling noses of each old dog.
The air is thick with whispers and jokes,
Where even old coats can crack yokes.

Starlit Refuges of Thought

Underneath a bed, dreams do hide,
Where lost toys await, with nowhere to slide.
Out of the window, a moth takes flight,
While the shadows dance with all their might.

Blankets pile high, a fort will bloom,
Where dragons roam in the living room.
Beneath the cushions, the secrets lay,
As the silence giggles and plans to play.

Pillows whisper tales of delight,
As dust bunnies dream of a glorious flight.
The night yawns wide, laughter escapes,
In a symphony made of old tapes.

Stars chuckle down from the sky,
As they peek through the window with a sigh.
Antique lamps blink like winking eyes,
Sharing stories of moonlit skies.

Clocks That Stopped Long Ago

Tick-tock? More like tick-snooze,
These clocks are playing games with views.
Time forgot, but not the snacks,
As biscuits waltz on the shelf, in packs.

Old toys sit on a shelf so grand,
Plotting a coup with a rubber band.
A dinosaur winks at a dusty book,
While the old cat gives a clever look.

Pendulums swing in perpetual jest,
While memories take occasional rest.
The gears may rust, but laughter's bright,
Filling the room with pure delight.

Tangled wires form art divine,
As clocks giggle in perfect rhyme.
Minutes and hours, they play a game,
Unbothered by the world's dull claim.

Boxes of Echoed Laughter

In a box labeled 'never opened,'
Sit echoes of joys, and chatter unbroken.
Marbles clink with a sly delight,
While invisible friends plan a night.

A tuba toots from a corner dark,
While the socks play tag with a spark.
The echo of giggles fills the air,
As if old toys just don't care.

A jumble of crayons, colors to share,
Creating rainbows everywhere.
Puppets are dancing without a string,
This attic's alive with the joy it brings.

Boxes filled with whispers and cheer,
Every creak is a laugh to hear.
Memories play hopscotch on the floor,
In this sanctuary, love does soar.

Between the Beams of Memory

In corners where the shadows play,
I found a hat that wore a sway.
It danced around, a jaunty fling,
Claiming it was once a king.

Beneath the light, a dustball rolled,
With tales of mischief yet untold.
It winked at me, a cheeky sprite,
Saying, 'Dance with me tonight!'

A shoe that squeaked in glee and pride,
Claimed it could jump like a bunny wide.
I laughed aloud, and so we spun,
A two-step jig, oh, what fun!

A spider waved, all eight in tow,
Said he'd put on a funny show.
With webs that trapped a thought or two,
I clapped my hands and laughed anew.

Tattered Pages of Possibility

Old books flip open with a grin,
Each tale begins with where it's been.
A storybook of socks gone mad,
Where mismatched pairs make mothers sad.

I read of lemons playing ball,
And sugar ants who hold a brawl.
The pages turned with every quirk,
As parsnips showed their dance, berserk!

A bookmark slipped, a rhythmic pirouette,
Giggling as it landed wet.
I spilled some tea on tales of woe,
But laughter brewed, and off we go!

To dream of cows that play the lute,
Who wear bright hats – oh, how they toot!
Each chapter bursts with silly schemes,
A world awash with tangled dreams!

A Ballet of Whimsical Whispers

In the nook where shadows twirl,
Socks pirouetted, giving a whirl.
A broomstick joined, with bristles long,
Swaying gently to a tune of song.

A teapot tapped its spout in glee,
With melodies from old, wise glee.
Each cup and saucer took their place,
In a dance where laughter filled the space.

Tiny moths dressed up for a ball,
Under the moon, they'd spin and sprawl.
Their wings a flurry, bright and clear,
Chasing giggles, inviting cheer!

With every flutter, a secret shared,
Of dreams that soar and hearts prepared.
In this ballet of joyful sounds,
Silly surprises in leaps abound!

Chests of Starlit Fantasies

In a wooden box, I found a shoe,
Claiming the right to dance with dew.
It wore a smile, all shiny bright,
Said it could moonwalk on a starry night.

A jingle bell, with wishes afloat,
Declared it built a wishing boat.
Sailing on dreams of buttered toast,
It made me laugh, oh, how I boast!

A chestnut squirrel with nuggets of gold,
Recited tales of adventures bold.
I joined in with claps and wild shouts,
As dreams unraveled in joyful bouts!

With every drawer pulled out a sight,
Of grooviness and sheer delight.
In the treasure trove where giggles gleam,
Life's a wild, whimsical dream!

A Tapestry of Random Thoughts

In corners where treasures might rest,
A sock puppet holds an impromptu fest.
He tells tales of socks long misplaced,
With giggles and wiggles, they joyously raced.

A jigsaw that's missing a crucial piece,
Cried out for help, but found no release.
The puzzle of life, an amusing charade,
With scattered shapes and plans badly made.

Old comic books bursting with flair,
Heroes and villains in mid-air stare.
They play chess with the dust bunnies' kin,
As laughter erupts, we both grin.

That old typewriter, rattling away,
Scribbles nonsense, yet here it will stay.
Papers of whims, absurd dreams untold,
In a world of wonders, both silly and bold.

Fleeting Glances from Above

From the beams overhead, you might spy,
A dust-mite ballet under a blue sky.
They twirl and they spin, such grace in the air,
While the candles sneeze and the shadows declare.

A clock with no hands counts moments of fun,
It giggles at time as if it's a pun.
Each tick is a tickle, each tock is a cheer,
While the cobwebs hang out and sip on their beer.

Old hats hang out, plotting grand schemes,
To take over lawns, or at least steal some beams.
With feathery trims and a wink on the side,
They'll dance in the twilight, nowhere to hide.

A breeze through the skewed boards whispers my name,
Crackling with secrets and a touch of the tame.
So come grab a laugh from what's covered in dust,
In a world that delights, oh, you know, it's a must!

Saga of Forgotten Toys

A toy soldier stands on a pile of old books,
With a crown made of rubber bands and strange hooks.
He plots a revolt with a stuffed teddy bear,
While marbles in corners giggle unaware.

The checkers and chessmen are lost in grand lore,
Plotting epic battles on the creaky floor.
When the sun peeks in, they all rise to decree,
This kingdom's hilarious—a royal jubilee!

Lego bricks form castles with doors made of cheese,
As elves play poker with the old game of keys.
In the midst of a quest for candy and cake,
They find endless laughter at each silly mistake.

From shadows they chant and clap without pause,
For a rubber duck is their savior—applause!
In the realm of retreat, chaos reigns supreme,
With giggles and snorts, it's all just a dream.

The Flicker of Distant Epiphanies

A lightbulb flickers, an idea takes flight,
As the broomsticks dance in the pale moonlight.
Ideas get tangled in webs of delight,
With hiccups of laughter, they take to the night.

The feathers from hats have a tale of their own,
Whispering secrets in the night's monotone.
As masks throw a ball in their finest disguise,
The giggles grow louder, the ceiling replies.

Distant thoughts echo, bouncing like balls,
While the cozy old blanket forever enthralls.
He dreams of a trip to candy cane shores,
With a giggle from cats as he opens the doors.

So let's toast with mugs filled with frothy delight,
To the funny adventures we've chased in the night.
As the shadows of laughter entwine and embrace,
In a world of odd wonders, we all find our place.

A Port of Dreams Abandoned

Once a ship sailed on thoughts so bright,
Now it's stuck under dust, out of sight.
Where treasures of laughter have drifted away,
Barrels of giggles, all lost in the fray.

The sails hang low, like my hapless dreams,
Fish stories are whispered, some might be memes.
A parrot named Chuck now works at the bar,
His tales of the sea, are quite bizarre.

Uncle Tim's cap sits with crumbs of the past,
He claims it once flew by a sea monster vast.
How did it end up in this creaky old place?
A ship full of oddities, lost in space!

So let's gather courage and board this old ship,
With laughter as sails, on a comical trip.
Together we'll jaunt through the jests of the past,
In the port of lost dreams, we'll party at last!

Secrets That Linger in Silence

In corners where whispers of dust tend to dance,
Lies the odd sock that dreamed of romance.
It's paired with a shoe that believes it can fly,
While crickets convene with a curious sigh.

A mysterious box claims it holds the key,
To laughter and secrets, oh what could they be?
Rumors of gnomes that once resided here,
Attempting to drink all the juice from a pier!

A sticky old note—the handwriting's a mess,
It reads, "Send help! I'm trapped with this stress!"
But it's just old Aunt Edna with cookies galore,
Baking up dreams that we can't help but adore.

So let's rummage through silence, uncover old cheer,
As we giggle at treasures tucked neatly in here.
Each secret still waits, with a soft little grin,
In the corners of whispers, let the fun begin!

The Celestial Archive

In a dome full of stars that forgot how to shine,
There sits a collection of cosmic wine.
A comet once swirled in a dance so divine,
But tripped on a planet, now uses a recline.

Each file holds a tale that's wacky and grand,
Of aliens who visited, but lost their band.
With disco lights flashing, they crooned 'til they dropped,
In a galaxy far, where time just got flopped.

A moon made of cheese is quite proud of its age,
But one bite from a cat turned it right to a sage.
The asteroids giggle at comets so brash,
As sunbeams throw parties, but they always clash.

Let's sift through the stars, let our laughter erupt,
At the weirdness in space, we're all strangely cup-'d.
With cosmic confetti flying high in the night,
In this celestial archive, everything feels right!

A Melodie of Memory's Pieces

An old record spins with a scratch and a pop,
Singing tales of the past, will it ever stop?
Nostalgia trips lightly on shoes that are worn,
While dances of yesteryears couple and mourn.

Marbles and crayons all hide in plain sight,
Under layers of giggles that brighten the night.
A trumpet says "toot!" from a far dusty nook,
While the accordion whispers—come check out my book!

Each piece holds a story, a laugh just in time,
With thoughts that bounce wildly, not stuck in a rhyme.
Let's gather the fragments of silly delight,
And assemble a symphony that's pure and bright.

So let's play this melody, a mix-match of fun,
With echoes that linger, our joy has begun.
For in this grand concert of whimsical sights,
We'll dance through the memories, embracing delight!

Whispers of Enchantment in the Dark

In shadows where the dust bunnies dance,
A sock puppet prince takes a chance.
He juggles old keys with a grin,
A party for moths, come join in!

The broom in the corner starts to hum,
To tunes of a world where the fairies drum.
Each creak of the floorboards, a joke so sly,
As the laundry hangs out and waves goodbye.

A book with a spine that's bent and cracked,
Whispers of stories that time has lacked.
The cat with a hat starts to tell,
How he conquered the night, oh so well!

With teacups of laughter, spills in the gloom,
A gathering of spirits in every room.
Who knew a closet could hold such charm?
With giggles and tales that do no harm!

Fragments of a Silenced Song

The ukulele waits for a strum so bold,
In corners where secrets of cabbage are told.
Dust gathers on notes, a polka so sweet,
But the mice have a dance party, a real treat!

Lopsided shelves hold dreams made of cheese,
An orchestra of ants plays with ease.
Each rhythm a laugh, each note a cheer,
While the rubber bands stretch from ear to ear.

A hat with a feather sings out of tune,
But it's the best concert under the moon.
Bottles of laughter clink and explode,
As paper planes zoom down the road!

In the chaos of fun, the silence outplayed,
Each moment a whisper, a serenade.
So let the old toys and trinkets belong,
In the world of fragments where all sing along!

Hidden Worlds Beneath the Roof

A treasure trove of mismatched socks,
And rubber ducks with clocks like rocks.
The cobwebs giggle from their high perch,
As the lanterns flicker, join the search!

A napkin from a feast with crumbs,
Holds tales of tigers that once were drums.
With each little mystery tossed and thrown,
Lies a kingdom that is all its own.

The old chess set has seen better days,
Yet knights in creaky armor still play.
They make room for fun in every nook,
Unraveling stories from the dusty book.

The laughter echoes, the cheer is grand,
In this hidden world where dreams expand.
So take a dive into the whimsy rife,
For beneath the roof lies the zest for life!

A Sanctuary of Unraveled Wishes

In corners hushed where whispers bloom,
A hat made of wishes spins a tune.
It tickles the thoughts that float like fluff,
Juggling the wishes—oh, isn't that tough?

A teddy bear's conference, make no mistake,
Discussing the pillows, the dreams that they make.
With fluff balls bouncing, laughter ignites,
In a fortress of giggles, the fun ignites.

Do toys have a secret? You bet they do!
They're crafting a plan for a dance debut.
The cereal box sings with a quack,
As the spoons organize their dancing pack.

Jars of confetti and glitter galore,
Invite the old buttons to dance on the floor.
With dreams unraveled, joy takes the stage,
In this sanctuary of love and age!

Relics of Resilient Heartbeats

Old toys gather dust, a tale to tell,
A rubber ducky sings, 'I'm doing swell!'
Forgotten shoes dance, in a silent show,
While a sock puppet dreams of fame, don't you know?

Jars of pickles and marbles align,
Whispers of laughter, a sweet old wine.
The clock chimes loudly, its hands twist and twirl,
As memories jog with a glittering swirl.

A bear made from threads, with a button eye,
Winks at the stories where lost things fly.
Underneath the rafters, a chair gives a moan,
Sighing for journeys it once called its own.

Echoes of yesteryears bounce off the walls,
A cat in the corner, purring, it sprawls.
The attic's a carnival, of dreams gone amok,
A canvas of chaos that time forgot!

The Symphony of Forgotten Sighs

Dust bunnies dance to a scratchy old tune,
A tricycle laughs at the light of the moon.
A paper airplane boasts of its flight,
While an old radio crackles with delight.

Balloons from birthdays now shriveled and small,
Recite poetry softly, recalling it all.
A teapot with memories, steaming with glee,
Remembers the clamour of company.

Cinder block chairs support dreams made of fluff,
While toys have a rumble, declaring enough!
Marbles like starlight, roll wild on the floor,
Painting the shadows with stories of yore.

With slippers that giggle, and shadows that dart,
The symphony hums in a curious heart.
Every sigh of the past, a note to be played,
In the gallery of giggles, where memories parade!

Moonlit Journeys into the Past

A suitcase awaits, filled with quirks of old,
Maps of forgotten lands, stories untold.
Bicycle adventures, charmers of fate,
Winking at mischief, oh, it's never too late!

Ghosts of adventures with spaghetti hair,
Sashay in the stillness, a whimsical flair.
A compass that spins, laughing in vain,
Mapping the dance of the old candy cane.

Jars filled with giggles, and secrets galore,
Illuminated dreams behind every door.
Moonlight runs wild, on pillows of fluff,
Tickling nostalgia, saying, 'Just enough!'

Teddy bears whisper of escapades bright,
While the clock leans in, 'Hold on tight!'
In every lost button, laughter we find,
As we journey through memories, whimsical and blind!

Whimsical Thoughts Upon the Beams

Past hat stands are grinning, holding their ground,
With quilted smiles hidden, joy to be found.
An umbrella's arguing with a moth in flight,
Over who wears the colors of the night!

Dusty book spines lean in for a chat,
While the broom softly giggles, 'I'm not a doormat!'
A clock with a hiccup keeps time with a twist,
As shoelaces tangle, it can't be dismissed.

Tinkling of laughter, a madcap spree,
Amongst the forgotten, there's never a fee.
In the rafters' embrace, where dreams have a peek,
Whimsical thoughts frolic and cheekily sneak!

Old photos wink, like mischief untold,
Cozy and crooked, they gather the bold.
In a world made of beams, the magic will gleam,
As long as we cherish each whimsical dream!

Puzzles in the Dust

In the corners, toys conspire,
Mismatched socks and lost attire.
A puzzle piece found with glee,
Now fits a cat's face—who could see?

A dinosaur lurks beneath a book,
Whispering secrets with a crooked look.
Toaster's dancing, bread's in flight,
Who knew leftovers could be such a delight?

Dust bunnies plot a grand retreat,
With carrot sticks as their main treat.
A world of laughter, odd and bright,
Hiding in shadows, out of sight.

Join the fun, let's take a glance,
At the wild parties of dust's dance.
With giggles crawling, time bends,
In this attic, laughter never ends.

Dreams Hovering in the Rafters

Ninja squirrels with acorn swords,
Plan their heists in whispered cords.
While rubber ducks on the shelf conspire,
To take the plunge and build a fire.

Floating hats with eyes agleam,
Wave to us like a silly dream.
They tell of days when they could fly,
Before we tossed them up to the sky.

A tea party full of mismatched mugs,
And marching ants in endless hugs.
They dance upon the creaky beams,
Twisting together, plotting schemes.

What fun we have in this silly space,
With giggles echoing in this place.
The humor hides in shadows wide,
In all the dreams that here abide.

The Hidden Symphony of Ideas

A trumpet made of empty cans,
Is waiting for the music gangs.
While paperclip bands break out in song,
Oh what a noise! You can't go wrong!

The broomsticks sway to rhythm divine,
As noodles dance on the countertop line.
A cereal box spins, keeping score,
Of all the giggles echoing from the floor.

With noodles drumming, bowls in a row,
This hidden world puts on a show.
Pepper shakers join with a jerky jig,
As every item takes a big swig.

What a concert crafted from scraps,
Where ideas flow and never collapse.
In this crazy symphony we find,
The laughs and giggles intertwined.

Memories Spun in Cobwebs

Cobwebs drape like old man's hair,
Holding whispers of long-lost flair.
A teddy bear with one button eye,
Hides secrets of the days gone by.

The stack of letters, all unopened,
Ready to spill what love once coped in.
A sock puppet peeks from the gloom,
Wondering where's its other half's room.

Old board games call for a chance,
To relive the days of chance and dance.
With laughter echoing from the past,
These cobwebbed memories hold steadfast.

So dust off the treasures lost in time,
And join this attic's playful rhyme.
For every corner's packed with stories,
In webs of laughter, past glories.

Stories Woven in Shadows

In corners lurk the tales untold,
Like socks that lost their way, so bold.
A pirate's hat and rubber duck,
Plot twists waiting, just for luck.

Old teddy bears plot a heist,
With action figures, they won't think twice.
While dusty books giggle in delight,
As shadows dance in the soft moonlight.

A clock that ticks in jumbled rhyme,
Joins in laughter, a waste of time.
Each creak and groan a punchline shared,
In this realm of dreams, none are scared.

Behind those chests, hide secrets bright,
With whispers wrapped in the blanket of night.
Crispy chips and forgotten haste,
Living it up in this playful space.

A Bazaar of Old Aspirations

In a nook, a sign reads, 'Dreams for Sale',
With prices marked by a ghostly wail.
A tricycle that can't find a rider,
And glasses that make the world much wider.

The old chess set plays itself, you see,
With pieces gossiping as they disagree.
While mismatched shoes play hide and seek,
Underbed monsters take a peek.

A wishing well without the wish,
Where all the lost socks gather for bliss.
A game of hopscotch on an old rug,
With laughter woven in every tug.

Odd ambitions on display, so grand,
Like a googly-eyed, dancing band.
Each silly trinket a lost regret,
In this bazaar, there's no need to fret.

The Keeper of Silent Reflections

In mirrors cracked, stories collide,
With silent giggles they cannot hide.
An old shoehorn tells tales of woe,
As lipsticks plot a vibrant show.

Dust settles on a gleaming comb,
While daydreams wander far from home.
Pantomime ghosts in feathered hats,
Dancing with bemused old cats.

Postcards flutter like messy dreams,
Of beaches, rainbows, and bubbling streams.
Yet here they sway, in moonlit game,
Bearing secrets too shy to name.

The keeper chuckles from her chair,
With all these treasures, who can compare?
She jots down laughs 'neath a cozy quilt,
As echoes of joy from memories built.

Lantern Light on Dusty Shelves

A lantern flickers with stories old,
Casting shadows on treasures, bold.
Cans of marbles and strings of beads,
Whisper tales of forgotten deeds.

Beneath the dust, the laughter hums,
While invisible friends play thumb wrestling drums.
The dusty clock winks with a grin,
Tick-tock giggles where dreams begin.

An old broom bristles with magic tunes,
As it sweeps away all the afternoon's moons.
With rubber bands that stretch for miles,
And odd-shaped ghosts that tease with smiles.

Each flicker, a promise of joy to find,
Wrapped in the quirks of a playful mind.
In this realm of echoing sparks,
Where silliness dances and laughter embarks.

The Ghosts of Lost Imagination

In a corner sits a hat so bright,
A ghostly cat jumps, what a sight!
With a wink and a smile, he prances around,
Chasing shadows that haven't been found.

Old sketches scribbled on crumpled sheets,
Do they giggle or play little tricks?
Each doodle whispers tales untold,
Of fanciful creatures and adventures bold.

Mismatched socks dance in pairs with flair,
In this bonkers kingdom, no one has a care.
Jars of jelly beans sing lullabies sweet,
As the phantom chef prepares silliness to eat.

Bouncing ideas on pogo sticks high,
Silly things float like clouds in the sky.
With a flick of a wand made of bendy straws,
Imagination reigns with chuckles and oohs.

Adventures in the Cobwebbed Heights

Up in the rafters, a jester resides,
With rubber chickens and googly-eyed rides.
Spinning his tales from dust-covered scrolls,
He juggles the laughter that tickles our souls.

Each cobweb is threaded with stories of old,
Where spiders weave fables worth more than gold.
A pirate ship sails on said threads so gray,
With capering pirates who dance the night away.

Old clocks giggle when the hour strikes two,
Telling time tales that are silly but true.
A teapot squeaks like a mouse on the run,
As it brews up a party, oh what fun!

The ceiling fan whirls like a merry-go-round,
While dust bunnies flip and dance all around.
In this whimsical realm, no reason to pout,
Join the ruckus, shout laughter out loud!

The Lullaby of Old Treasures

Under a blanket of dust they lay,
Old toys and trinkets come out to play.
A puppet croons silly tunes from the past,
Making the hours fly by oh-so-fast!

A clockwork bird chirps in a squeaky tone,
Her wings made of paper, she'd never flown.
With a tap dance from plush bears in the night,
They giggle till dawn in a most jolly sight.

In dusty corners, old comics do fight,
With caped heroes saving sleep from the night.
Bubblegum dreams float around like balloons,
As treasure chests hum their jazzy old tunes.

Under the stars made of twinkling lights,
Adventures await in these vibrant nights.
With every laugh, a memory is spun,
Resting in treasures, oh what fun is begun!

Flight of the Imaginary Wings

A paper airplane soars with glee,
Wings made of wishes, flying wild and free.
It loops and twirls past a wooden toy bear,
Whispering secrets of joy in the air.

Brittle dreams float on glittery streams,
As pigs with aviator goggles chase beams.
The rocket ship giggles, ready for flight,
Launching into laughter, igniting the night.

Dizzying thoughts swirl like confetti in breeze,
A parade of ideas dances with ease.
With each daring dive, imagination sings,
Creating a world where anything springs!

So let your dreams flap their wings and glide,
On the currents of giggles wherever they ride.
In this whimsical place, laughter takes flight,
Crafting a cosmos of fun, pure delight!

The Magic of Starlit Nostalgia

In the corner, a chair with a grin,
Dust bunnies dance, let the games begin.
Old socks are hanging, a delightful sight,
Whispering secrets in the soft moonlight.

Lampshades are giggling, casting strange beams,
Reflecting the laughter of forgotten dreams.
A rubber duck quacks, it's lost in the fun,
In the realm of shadows where we used to run.

Jars full of giggles, mismatched and bright,
They echo the echoes of our childhood flight.
Polaroid pictures flicker like stars,
Each moment a comet, each memory ours.

So let's climb those stairs with a skip in our feet,
Dance with old slippers, oh what a treat!
In the laughter and joy of this whimsical place,
We'll find our own magic; we'll reignite grace.

Memories Wrapped in Cobwebs

Cobwebs are blankets for things long forgot,
A sandwich from '89? It's lost in the lot.
Toys have their meetings, they whisper and plot,
One claims the treasure is an old coffee pot.

A clock with no hands is still ticking away,
Counting those moments from a bright summer day.
With echoes of giggles that linger like mist,
The lanterns are swaying, it's impossible to resist.

A thimble of laughter, a jar of old sighs,
Keep spinning the tales they hide with their lies.
The ghosts of our glory are roaming around,
In closets, they play hide-and-seek with the sound.

So let's leave our worries amidst all the fluff,
Embrace the weirdness, this place is enough.
With each laugh we share in this lovely old haunt,
We'll bask in the glow of a whimsical font.

A Canvas of Unwritten Stories

On the shelf, an easel with dreams yet to paint,
A gnome with a mustache that looks like a saint.
Each crayon's a wizard, casting colors so bright,
Imagination's spark ignites the delight.

Pages are crumbling, but words want to dance,
Hidden in stories, they leap at the chance.
An octopus reads while spinning a tale,
In the carnival chaos where ideas set sail.

Blank canvases giggle under layers of dust,
Awaiting the whispers of brushes and trust.
A rubber band ball spins wild through the air,
As the walls chuckle softly, lost in the flair.

So gather your dreams in a wild paper chase,
Let creativity bounce through this lively space.
With laughter and colors, the tales will unfold,
In the canvas of magic where laughter is gold.

Fleeting Fantasies in Dim Light

In a box of lost wishes, I find a balloon,
It pops with a giggle, oh what a tune!
Fairies and gnomes in a whimsical race,
Chasing the shadows of an old teddy's face.

Under the bed, a glimpse of a shoe,
Waltzing with dust bunnies, just me and you.
The socks sing a duet, a rather sweet sound,
While old forgotten dreams spin round and round.

Silly old lampshades throw light like a flare,
Illuminating visions that dance in mid-air.
In this realm of dim light, pure joy ignites,
As laughter emerges from the curious sights.

So let's twirl with the shadows, let our worries take flight,

In the fleeting embraces of whimsical night.
We'll spark all the echoes of what once could be,
In this land of mischief, so wild and so free.

www.ingramcontent.com/pod-product-compliance
Lightning Source LLC
Chambersburg PA
CBHW060126230426
43661CB00003B/348